Saturn is Mostly Weather

5/5/97

To Cathie,

Good to see you again
at these readings. Hope
your own poetry goes
well!

All best,

Gene

Saturn is Mostly Weather

Selected & Uncollected Poems

GENE FRUMKIN

CINCO PUNTOS PRESS  EL PASO, TEXAS

Acknowledgements

Many thanks are due to the following publications in which some of these poems originally appeared: "Festival of the Wolves" in *Albuquerque Living*; "The Game Refuge" in *The Amicus Journal*; "Young Woman, Much Older Man" in *Cafe Solo*; "Maps" in *Caliban*; "The Singer of Manoa Street" in *The Chariton Review*; "The Moon at Canyon de Chelly" in *Dacotah Territory*; "Salmon in the Pool" and "Above Taos" in *Floating Island IV*; "Origins" in *Hawaii Review*; "Weather and the Quiet Stars" in *Literary Arts Hawaii*; "Father to Son" and "At Such Times" in *New Letters*; "Correlating a Woman" in *The Paris Review*; "Saturn Is Mostly Weather" and "After Reading Some Poems by William Bronk" in *Poetry Northwest*; "The Armada," "Jackdaw" and "What Was Left Behind" in *Practices of the Wind*; "The Inexcusable" in *Puerto del Sol*; "The Brown Dog" in *Sulfur*; "The Mandelstam Poems"in *Tarasque I*; and "Stages in Assembling a Mirror" in *Tyuonyi*.

"George Ruth's Middle Name" reprinted from *Yankee Magazine*, published in Dublin, New Hamshire.

Photo of Gene Frumkin © 1990 by Cynthia Farah
Photos of Saturn © 1992 by Richard Baron

FIRST EDITION

ISBN 0-938317-16-4
Library of Congress Catalog Card Number 91-072301

This book is funded in part by generous support from the National Endowment for the Arts. The author also gratefully acknowledges the assistance of the Virginia Center for the Creative Arts for its support in the preparation of this book.

*Cover design, typography and book design
by Vicki Trego Hill of El Paso, Texas*

Printed on acid-free paper
∞

Contents

from Clouds and Red Earth

Uncollected Poems

In memory of
Thomas McGrath

Salmon in the Pool

That was the earlier dream
in which I walked to the pool's edge
where one fish, a cloudy salmon,
tried to swim upstream. Of course
the pool's blue walls would not allow it.
I remembered saying, "There is
no stream." Later someone told me
the salmon was clearly
myself.
         In the next dream
I was more reasonable. I stayed inside,
in my room, painting maps
on my walls in daring colors.
All of the maps resembled Africa
and I knew why even while I painted.
I wanted to go away, to become
my most ancient ancestors.
                    Now
someone tells me I have gone
too far in locking my windows
against the light. I swim inside
myself. I draw charts for retirement
from all obligations, including
love. "You rationalize everything,"
she says. "You think
like a system."
           Or a salmon, I think,
on its way across the Atlantic
to the great Red Sea. Yes,
I am repressed, as everyone is
who draws reason from movie-lot
walls. Even so, against death
and toward it, I tug
at the many shores where wisdom lives,
I pull the groaning water with me.

The Brown Dog

Brown dog frozen to the side
of a brick building, half a floor up.
His dead muzzle whimpers in wind
that comes from Lake Ontario or another water
nearer to us. We are children, our job
to scrape the dog off that brick
even as his head, still not stiffened
to the body, quivers lightly, nodding.
                                              Eyes
open, we notice, darkly alight, living
in the frozen morning. We wonder, I'm sure,
how the dog climbed the several feet
of brick wall, how it happened
that the frost so meticulously
caught him mid-step. Where was he going
that night in mid-October when
nothing in the air confirmed a
deathly cold?
                  Almost, we thought,
as if the dog were paper. We stayed back,
not frightened but wishing for the sun
to brighten, to warm up. Who had assigned us
this task? Maybe he would rise in the breeze,
lofted by our imagination into the hole
of another mystery.
                        She and I waited,
children did I say? No, but frightened
of our years, their purpose in bringing us
this far, to see that brown dog, in its meaningless
mid-journey.
                  I take her cold hand.
My mind whimpers. Let's dig, she says, wherever
we can. I raise my shovel towards
the dog's feet, then lower it. No, I say,
some other time. She nods. The sun stays,
clinging to the same wall.

The Inexcusable

All his absences came to visit him, night
or day, his failure to be communicative,
to offer signs of care, and these absences
decline to honor him, to care about his
failure to mean anything at those times, of love
or death or even illness, when meaning
opens a way to be declared, simply,
in the best language available, or any language
that is meant.
                To offer white space
when the gradual eye lifts toward the supreme
vacancy, to offer a gap where a mouth should be,
a leaving of purest transparency where
an object might have filled someone's moment
with even the smallest something, even
as a voiced memory to the surviving of
living; to have been a shadow of love's
presence, this is to have left a subject
without act, the heart's grammar unlearned.

Father to Son

Don't remind me of the Chippewas.

                          My father's
teeth were stitched together by manycolored threads,
some of which were still dangling from his mouth
when I knew him.

                 He spoke in buttons,
each word had four holes.

                     So if he wasn't the Czar
of all the Russias, it doesn't make any difference.
They had fancy rubles then in his youth when the plums
had not yet wrinkled in his eyes, royal portraits
and every tint they could lay their hands on to ink
their minting machines. Nicholas, Alexander, Peter
the Great. Who cares if Catherine, also the Great,
fucked a horse.

               So when you remind me
of the Chippewas, I forget them right away.
I won't say anything about my mother, a saintly woman
who thought my father was an ex-Polish officer and married him
not in that Old Corpse of a World but right here
in the New One. The immigration officials couldn't spell
either of their names so when I finally got my father's
one cuff was too long.

                  As for the Chippewas,
you'll have to look them up in the Columbia Desk Encyclopedia, son,
or the Davy Crockett Almanac. I don't have all the answers,
just those that were left to mildew on the clothesline
forty years ago

               and are hanging there today

                         in perfect shape
like hostages executed for not tying their shoelaces.

The Mandelstam Poems

*One of the finest of all Russian poets, Osip Mandelstam—born in War-
saw in 1891—died in a Stalin prison camp in 1938 near Vladivostok,
according to the most reliable information. Born a Jew, Mandelstam
converted early to Christianity and was also at early odds with what he
perceived as the oppressive tendencies inherent in the Bolshevik Revolu-
tion. Most of the vital facets of his life and work are related by his widow,
Nadezhda Mandelstam, in her work, published in English in two volumes
under the titles* Hope Against Hope *and* Hope Abandoned. *These
poems were written while I was living in Honolulu.—G.F.*

I.

One spreads a situation
across the page. Suggestions of tallow
and stale beer. A license to rob the poor.
Who can say how chill it is in Voronezh now—
where M. once lived in exile?

Through the night birds croon
from the foliage. A shift, it seems,
in how we are to oblige
the governing system. Tropical rain. The women
all wear bikinis.

So, in this apartment, I overlook
Manoa Stream covered by the brown air
of mosquitoes. A policeman
might come. With an Oriental warrant
for my arrest. On charges.

Long ago, when I was a child,
his wife preserved. He had taken a position
on the cross and made humor under the guns
of the Lord. Otherwise no one could say
that the situation ever changed.

II.

Since it happened. I still wait
dumbstruck.
            Death closes its eyes.
No one dares to dream of glass
in the station at Maly Yaroslavets.

I will not go there. The worst
is not over. All of us
are exiles. Soon.
            That town
where M. did not live even a day,
blacked-out town, must be rubble by now.
Besides, how could I believe
in the cold?
            My body turns
on the spit of its own rage.
Its fat congeals in a bucket.
The nerves are bits of string
blackening atop innumerable candles.
What thought can there be for others
when the veins burn dry?

From the enchanted land
to paradise. A few months.
It seems like a vacation.
Then while I wait the train stops
at Maly Yaroslavets.
From dry heat to moist heat
to bones mirrored in death's eyes.

III.

How it comes together, one
cloud struggling into
another. Or a seam
crooked down the trouserleg.

Beauty not as you would have it,
classical, but arranged always
prematurely, one eye closed,
the other devout.

All right, M., we meet
in a black tunnel. A train
approaches, its cyclopean light
clogging our lungs

until only a breather of sun
could revise the actual. Zero,
however, is a fact of space:
a hole large enough for

2,000 Milky Ways. Had you so much
trust, M., in the Earth's
rainbows and Italian circles?
You and I pasted together

with frail glue on a Greek landscape,
your pipe crisp in my ear
like the morning birds
outside my window, here on this

other island where I live now
far from home, a single space away
from your death. Play on,
play on, heartless Pan:

let our balls roll free
to the music. The blood does not
congeal, it flows down the film
between our breaths. Play on.

IV.

Musician of the green heart,
a winter gone baying after stones,
so the mouth bleeds
in a cup   and henceforth
calls out only its own name.

Heart, mossy grown in its time,
warms in crusted blood,
its cry of wild geese
migrating across many years.
M., you are a clean vessel.

This print in saffron dust:
your crypt, heart, where you
have settled down stonily.
In Armenia. Where others
drink of you, leaf by leaf.

V.

Oh, M., these days when wine pours down
stone walls, the skies are alone, rabbis forget
their constellations. Who will pray
for a man lying devoutly in his hole
still smelling of greasepaint? From the East
no sacred friends may be seen
coming to our house.
                    Did you also
dip your hands in milk at twilight?
I pass a window and see your face
advertised for sale. Your name is a tool
stuck in my throat. We believe these days
in the profound blare
of disenchanted objects,
                            in creatures
whose hair is dyed cosmic orange. Order prevails

only in loud distortions. You, M.,
who bled for presence, a speech
for growth and decay, here are the nails
and hammer, here is
the motley wood. But though I meet you
in such stealthy times
                                    as you did not live through,
I must confess to bristles of joy
even without your apostles
or the gospeled flesh. My life,
so childishly forged by crayons, absorbs
the edges of your absence. Our winesap sun
dangles with good humor, like a useless toy,
over the western shore.

VI.

Of course we are both approximations.
You a smudged window staring into
my eyes, mouth half open, still
half speaking the hard Cyrillic darkness inside
the makeshift room where you died, heart banished
from too many years of hope,
then no more hope at all.
                                    And I, who reach
a hand toward the black icy glass,
I am afraid the boards will creak
when I embrace you, and that the sound
may startle us both into a false reunion.
Austere father, old M., I try to define
your image, the brittle bones of it,
while your depth drags me down,
                                    your soul
already made in its sharp negative, Moscow-framed.
Nothing I see or say quite fits
your shape. The domes of the cold Russian city
shine dull gold in my remembrance
of your always temporary home.

Warming over your life this while on Oahu,
I live too greenly in my skin, old shade.

VII.

Seeing your death in black print, M.,
I turn my head to the north, toward Barrow, Alaska,
the most Arctic pit of these United States. I light a candle
and dedicate it to Poland, even to the Pope.
We are all still imbedded in subways and stale cake,
we are dancers along the rim of a shrill crater—
whatever happens, we must go on flinging birds into the air.

But your death, M., in black print
is not the same as your poems: not as serious,
not as beautiful. It is not the same as the Red soldier
with hacked-off leg seen through a trainwindow
in last night's movie. A false mutilation, true, yet also
an unexpected knock on the heart's door at midnight,
then the opening to a searing wind, to a dank angel.

It comes to this: M.'s death in black print
is a comet whistling through the ages, heard of
though seen only once, long ago. The account arrives by freighter
from the widow's pen, cargo too fragile to unload.
I stand on the pier gazing skyward at the black words' light,
prose gleaming from its hold so hidden in depth
that M.'s death is all alone, a gnawing sliver of thought.

VIII.

The Christian soul is free, you said,
who were chained to the air. Your humor black
like last night's wick at moments when we whispered
(two secret Jews) our puffs of inflammable breath,
when we fought over some designs of speech,
conjuring flowers and bones from frozen earth.

Let us play chess again with only a clock
between us; not as now a bare table
and the stars. Who shall be White
and who Red? The squares are bits of geometry
for our minds to master. How freely they move
while our hands remain at our sides, still unthawed.

Those speechless hours I have spent
looking into the pool to see your face,
thin graying beard and 19th century eyes,
the lips almost virginal. You must see me too
as you peer out from the theological water
in which you wear your Church like a second body.

Are you really free or does some airless truth
still force you? Guide me, if you can, toward
that dark island where soul may discern its models
on earth. The lights go on all over Honolulu,
people begin to get drunk, and soon
I will place my ear to your poems' mouth.

IX.

His trochaic walk, assisted by a muted cane,
precedes me through the gate. Black velvet collar
stitched onto a plum-colored coat, plum trousers
stuffed into black boots. The man hobbles
to a loveseat in the garden and falls upon it
as I wait by the outdoor aquarium, my aunt's
in the garden where I was orthodoxly wed.
Goldfish, 26 years older, ease their way
like an alphabet through the water. And lemons
still blossom on the lemon tree.
                              He is 47,
the man I followed for many miles, his heart
moving awkwardly in his chest. This is the year
of his death, for which he dresses with care,

even pomp. My wife moves in his chest,
one weak beat then a stronger one for dying.
This garden is canopied in yesterday's light,
caught in the wineglass I crushed back then
in the grass; here where I reach to lift him up,
Osip the Russian poet. He will not rise,
he will rest with Lydia there.
                          They are a pair;
their brilliance compels me to pull down my lids
over those vanities, parodies of despair, that bring me
to my knees. I beg forgiveness, regarding Lydia
in M.'s countenance. I rub my hand across
his plums and hear again Mendelssohn's famous march.
Of course M. will not pronounce me: he will serve
only as the name whose cloud I trail, galloping
like a horse or a rabbi on stilts faltering toward
another air that ends in a more enduring love.
Dear M., he runs off with my wife even as I watch.

X.

As for women, he thought they should nurse
the winter in a man's bones, wash the costumes
of night, chase the ephemerals who crowd one's air,
speak like the family silver, be
little dippers for the firmament of soup.
A woman should think of the snow's depth,
the particular shade of summer green, gray shadows
in the nature of song, and be tragic enough
to die away when love sweeps by
beating its greedy wings.
                          Only Akhmatova, dyed
in suffering's pale gold, survived M.'s
anointment, to live on in her own voice,
not to be spoken for. Mourning Stalin's dead,
she became herself a requiem which M., included,
could not outlive.
                          He remains now

his widow's harvest. She has drawn up M.'s image
from depths hidden to history's wandering eye;
otherwise soul would have mouldered with skull.
He was paper in her exiled suitcase, many seasons
of manuscript and a poster on whispering walls.
After modeling for M.'s Christian Woman
Nadezhda washed the ghosts from his silvery pen
and ladled out his words like God's own stars.

XI.

That cunning young man, Mandelstam,
perhaps compared his poems to the snow around
Moscow, perhaps prophesied his own survival
when the iron spikes of his widow's words melted down,
then certainly fled into massive earth,
into cavelike verses, and a cross and a star.
He was a system of stern humor,
a portrait of summer inside winter, this young Paraclete
who traveled the rails of his thin lines
smoothly toward his death.
                              Now we hear from him
in letters, warm as the late-spring winds
that hammer the snow around Moscow into
indelible white periods. As if
he can't wait to settle down, to smoke another cigarette
in one more freezing room, as if he lived
in the attic where all of us leave our passing thoughts,
a room we only enter as we move
toward some other description of life.
                              A smart one,
Mandelstam, blowing his breath into his wife's
mouth, holding her youthful consumption in his eyes,
caressing her old age with improbable luxuries:
the bony fingers of his poems, his skull's delicate erasures.
Adroitly, he died before it was too late,
before speech became a comma bearing too much weight,
while the world was still a certain place.

The Game Refuge

A passage, this game refuge
near the center of a city growing
out of the sand. The fowl
are safe by this pond
near a great river. If we humans
could glide so silently
in our atmosphere, lift off
but not fly too far from our lives.
If we could see ahead
only to the next bracken-covered bank
and feel in our blood an endless
return to home.
                    No, the city grows
around us, the air dimming
with worn light. Heavier, this air,
weighted down by the fuel
that keeps us traveling on
and back, swift migrations
within defined parameters. The more we go
the further we incite a thoughtless need
to harry ourselves. To ask
of our own deadliness a refuge,
survival.
                    Green, abundant life
and feathered life. Mallard and duck,
this and the visiting geese
from Canada. Squirrels storing
their winter away. Bees thorough and full
in the buzzing.

A man comes
to look, to get away from his destiny
for an hour. He is distracted
by money and love. He is aware
of his death. Outside his mind
the city burns on from road to road:
another shape of wild life,
endangered. And he with it,
he in great numbers looks for
water, the lotus and red osiers,
somewhere set aside for use in passage,
time reset short of death,
that first thought edging on to the shore.

Festival of the Wolves

There is the music of the wolves.
They chant to one another
legends of meat and snow.
Their favorite skies are gray
and this music is very cold.

The wolves describe our fears
in narrowing circles.

Glacial fur.

Breath of
slit-open guts.
              Wolves.
They smell our bodies
in the Arctic storm.
                    They close in.
Their music. The dance
of their steaming eyes.
They are delighted!
                 How justly,
how exaltedly they live.

Stalin the Good

I dreamt that Stalin sat at table
with three others
    two blond children
and an outline
        Stalin's

small knife patted
the butter, his bread a child's
    hair, at his arm a jar
of marmalade
        When Stalin

smiled I saw
I'd forgotten his moustache
    and was about to
paste it on
        A warm

breeze brings me roses   I have accomplices
even during
    the hours of light and reason
My madness
        flourishes

The Party

There in the corner
                    two wounds
    are bleeding quietly
        to each other
In the center
of the room the talk
                    is tictactoe
        always ending
        in a tie
    A joke cracks open
the eggplant night
and it spatters
everybody's face
                    A virgin
        thinks it's a turd
        and screams
A bombardment of owls
silenced only by the first
cymbals of moon clattering
the pool
        The bodies compose
a sonata
        by Karlheinz Stockhausen

                        Inside
    the wounds
    have trickled under the sofa
    and will remain there
    in dust and darkness
            scabs for tomorrow's
            cleanup lady

Elsewhere kisses melt
in glasses
      Love swims in milky puddles
      The clock snores
      The DeKooning on the wall
tries to utter a human cry

            Upstairs
a tiger prowls the rooms
and soon will cross the border

The Old Jew

He touches a match to the old Jew's beard
laughs, calling them curls of smoke
(The Jew smells like a chicken plucked and singed
his age contributes to the joke)

Not Mephisto but a man in the street
a brown shirt his career
boots the hymn of his ear   People surround
this ritual he set / bonfire of hair

a night of parades and Party songs
The Jew smothers his beard
screaming, in his coat / the crowd lingers in his darkness
aimless now their candle disappeared

Variation on an English Calendar

for Glenna Luschei

Seven years since that banquet
in the Ozarks when I saw you
steal off to the water
                  You stripped
and bathed in Fowler's Creek
You laughed to catch me on the bank
naked, my sword hanging
                     from a bough
Our horses rubbed each other
beneath their maculate canopy It was
a prophecy from the English calendar
that hung in my father's tailor shop
Later I learned you played the harpsichord

Seven years and now I grow apples
in the Española Valley of New Mexico
I have two goats a rooster and hens
a duckpond
              My sword hangs
above the adobe fireplace
ashen with rust   I think of buying more land
where sheep might graze
                   Fowler's Creek
passed through last night when my sleep
was a regiment of footsteps
across dried leaves
               In the next room
you are playing an air by Purcell
on the harpsichord You catch my medieval ear
listening   and laugh / the same golden thread
unraveled from the same naked form
on that Ozark field
               We have liberated love
from the lion of romance, somehow
make it home, bleeding but calm

Drinking in the Lux

in memory of Steve Stroh

It was beer and tequila
at the Lux   two long nights
as we argued with Dante Alighieri
about the propriety of light
at the bottom of volcanoes   he contending
there was no circle for such light
a mere moon in a watery eyelid

The children of Juarez are hideous
their eyes are beasts
                                    hungry so young
they quiver in the entrails of tourists
who rarely know they've been so sneakily struck

Beatrice was Rosario the first night
Teresa the second   Rosario drank
orange juice but Teresa drank beer
Rosario was worth $10 but Teresa
only 9   Teresa insulted Gloria
in the middle of Gloria's grinding ass
Rosario was not there the second night
It was a student Antonio who
introduced us both   Dante was there
looking for Beatrice too, there at the Lux
He said there was no light in basements
We said in America there existed
flashlights   He hadn't heard of them
but said in basements dark was the proper motive

The children of Juarez sell
American cigarettes to Americans
They are hideous   not to be trusted

Two long nights quickly spent
to our last few dollars   Dante said
he was in exile from the sun

We noted it was night in any case   He said
we were all in exile   We began
to wonder   Teresa said he was a creep in Mexican
We smoked all the cigarettes Steve had bought
from the children of Juarez
Dante said the lighted tip of a cigarette
reminded him of Mount Etna
Old nostalgic divinity student, I thought
Next thing he'll be bawling
in memory of Benito Mussolini

The children of Juarez are minefields
I must remember to step around them
on tiptoe
                If I should touch one
I'd fly apart

All that drinking in the Lux
the dollars spent   This was
the bottom of something   the light
of something   We were dimmed and doused
two nights in a row   Only Dante
was clear   As we walked to our hotel
I said, "Observe the celestial affluence"
while pointing to the ground
A lady named Beatrice halted
as we passed   "Can't you guys
walk straight?"   "The light of Dante
is blinding us," Steve said   "More likely
it's the dark," said Beatrice   who was in her 40s
accompanied by three male adults

We flew to the Hotel San Antonio
like falling stars
                that last night
glad the children of Juarez were all asleep

Stopping at the Ramada Inn
in Kingman, Arizona

Whenever, these days, I go to California by car
I pause overnight at the Ramada Inn
in Kingman, Arizona There the carpets are not of wool
so I don't wake up with a headache The corpses are the same
the ones I'm used to   Their faces are greeny yellow
as the camera works and plays But corpses still
Not much change in their position, even in Kingman
A man named Dave Nichols, I think, from Phoenix
is their local representative Corpses too
need their livewire man   Believe me, I'm sold
on the whole fantasy, every scale-inch of it

The room in the Ramada is obtrusively clean
glasses wrapped in paper, instant coffee if I want it
and no headache in the morning I have faith
in those corpses, that they exist Precisely dead
as Dave Nichols softsells them   I like that
His own face yellowy green, not like Earthmen's blue
A true vicar of the awesome dead I feel comfortable
in colorful Kingman In the Ramada Among my neighbors

Pulsar

swarms, tides   The forever of dead stars
pulsing through opaque space   temp, sound
We place a stethoscope to Cosmic body
and hear these signals   their impossible mass
the universe a Bach score, each note
weighing 50 million tons, the counterpause
perhaps even more

                    One star in the small galaxy
designated NGC 5253 is Kowal's supernova
60 billion miles from Earth   It is now flowering
(May 26, 1972) as the nuclear bomb does
consuming its entire system of hydrogen and helium so brightly
it obscures everything else in its world
The finale, only a few weeks to cross   the star
wilted, dried of all radiance   soon the funeral march
forever the signal, forever the pause

Is it dead if it shines no more
though we hear it?
               Is Bach dead?
Their life, I think, is immanent hair
the hair of their light growing in the grave

The Present Is Timeless
& Vice-Versa

When the moment steals
the watch from your wrist
what you have done before
is lost, what you will do
forgotten
        This moment is water
and you lave yourself
in its darkest fathoms
You see only the water
Your eyes are crystalline
You love yourself
without limit
        in this moment
which has its walls
its floor and ceiling
Sooner or later
you remember something
It's always sad

Later you'll remember
this moment   It also will be sad
How you loved yourself then
and not quite now

When another moment steals
the watch from your wrist
and you swim for your life
the "now" is absent
Your life is in the sun
No shadows cling to it

Later you observe again
the shadow of yourself
you are no longer
here
　　　This moment
was stolen from you,
as always
　　　　　You are sad to be
worth no more
than the watch on your wrist
You are sad to be
the shadow of yourself
whom you love, the shadow-lover
you who are able
to doze within the sun
though briefly
and without notice

Household

it gets dusty   dust on bookcases
on phonograph the floor   blotches on the floor
dust on windowsills the wainscots
stains on formica table   dust on watercooler
on gasheater   blotches on refrigerator stove sinkcounter
dust on stuffed chairs   blotches on windows
stains in the sinks   dust in rugs mattresses
on lampshades   stains on the blinds
dust on typewriter papers books
stains in rivulets on kitchen walls
under everything blotches into stains
into everything   entropy doesn't pause
in pursuit of the maculate   it aims
has design   it wants to be a leopard
and to leap across the chasm
between here and now   this bronze leap, forever spotless
One move to cleanse these wounds
       one move...

As Hares Nibble at Young Cherry Trees

Between the air and the white spaniels
there is little to square   as also the spruce
in this laundry   getting clean
How within and outwith the boundary labors
so Eiseley's Split where one is seen
in another language   loud with names
never silenced before   Lauds, then
for the archangel of summer snow
and honor to the chapel fallen
below the earth

             Of time we have enough
never had so much truth   not since
the last letter from Pleistocene
Crap on that woolly log, System
Opt for the better view   that which is
both fabulous and on cue

             Polanyi
you shithead, when Bukharin farted in your face
he learned how to die head-on
though you, lovely cockroach, possess
grace, thought's quick pace
and money left over for another crash

The spruce are white now, the spaniels
green   Small enough accomplishment
for an hour at Easy Wash   the less done
the more intent remains   Lauds
for Equatorial Africa and the chimneys
of Spain
             Out of all this organized
slaughter surely one line is worth
believing   A human arm
dangles from the surprised clock
whose alarm has left for the day

Vines

Vines   with clusters of white buds   nudge one another
warp around one another   within our bodies   These vines
are ligaments of sleep   They are green with white buds
and in the sunlight are still and patient   whatever life
they have is looming around their simple discipline:
to touch lightly   to rub quietly to coil about   as the sunlight
reaches into them   within our bodies   We are spoken to
the vines speak and say no words   it is their tongues
we hear   subtle vibrations of the buds   no more
than sprigs of whiteness floating down our arms and legs
Our blood billows in this languor   as if to set sail
across unforeseeable seas   The whiteness of sleep
which these vines sprout forth is also tied
to our bodies   ready to lift us from our leaden stopping-pace
loft us upward   we are but a breath away from flying
The secret of our vines is helium   they are filaments
of helium   Our bodies moor them so firmly to the ground
they avenge themselves on us   sigh into us their heavy petals
their curvatures a silky music   three slow notes
that repeat themselves monotonously   in,out,around   in,out,around
That is all we can hear   in,out,around   The vines within us
surround us   We observe them ceaselessly even as they
embrace us   caressing, wooing   It is easy to swoon
as lovers are said to do   The white buds smell of honey
of apples of lumber   their fragrances exhaust our senses
We   who could fly as quickly as breathe   hands bound for love
behind our backs feet racing to the moon in hardcaked ice
Vines nudge one another   warp around one another
say "sleep, sleep"   We open our eyes to the darkness within
The stars hang firmly down from their sky   If we caught one
its skin would be pocky, cool and lightly green   it would break
as our teeth and nails dug in   Our body in air
sucked out of its immobile cloud / suckled into
the lime-orchard, green and swift: sea without waves

The Mouth

Inside my mouth the brown hide of a bear
the clumsy hustle quick sweep of paw
rip of claws   It's an awkward tool to cut out
holes in space   By the time I'm done for the day
there is often no sanctuary for my head
only enough carved for a single eye
and then it's winter   a need to close my mouth

whispers, saliva   This rugged fur enclosed
within a membrane thin as those ghosts
that were exhaled, raw, into icier winds than anyone
now remembers   My bear
trapped inside a thicket of maplesap, rumbles
thrashes about   A fresh warmth coats his heart
Today the sun is exactly the size
of the moon   Bear licks his paw
and my mouth covets the forest of honey

A movement of lips   I savor what the sun
has brought   just a speck of sweet dust
The heaviness, a thick mass, lumbers into my throat
and sticks to the walls   The honey is frozen
Bear yawns   What can the tongue see now?

Over and over, the cold sleep

On the Ground

You advance ever closer
on hands and knees   the gurgle
the primal drool   You're at it again
rubbing your lips into the rug
to taste green wool red wool gold wool
dust of numberless footsteps
the heaviness of sunmotes
that lay down at last to rest

The flesh absorbs
all inquiry   is in its trust
stratum and priest of the black forest
the crystalline lake

Wallow roughly in wellsprings
let mud seep through
your noseholes   sneeze out
the boogie-men   smell those bones
vanished even from Earth's bowels
swallow those cries
that cracked the arctic ice
ecstatic groans little more
than sprouting animals

On your knees you little prick
when you philosophize
When you part the lips
praise the snail
Make love on your knees
to god's Japanese dragon
tattooed green red and gold onto
the carpet-grail   Suck up the dust
clean it all up   Culture
is on the ground all ways the ground

Water Berries

Water berries   the salted and sweet
those that grow above the trees
and those that wait slowly
beneath the soil   water berries
in Delphi's mouth   water berries
in Thoreau's journal in the tails
of the four horses of Venice
and in the crowded forum
where the voters applaud their peril

Water berries at the source of candles
cloister of albino worship   chosen
by all assassins   ocher berries
berries of indigo and of the frost
that burns in the sun   Flavor
of igneous rock of ivy and bog
of peacock juice   Berries that melt
and berries that harden in the womb
berries that work and berries that sleep

Water berries blacken without reason
and glow with dim orange light
through the fogs of heart, high tides
of bloodbeat   water berries fulfill
all regions of Cosmic body: stars
and buds   magnets and fingernails
Water berries cluster in the form
hidden behind your life   the framed morning
the smoke of your words at night

In Memory of My Frank O'Hara

                    Your feelings
fetched a low price in that
garage sale   The orange-&-pink
bowl-style lampshade with fringes
brought you however a pissoir
in Paris   You had never liked
that shade nor its lampbase
(a female nude molded
in white plastic front and rear)
The pissoir is blue with a live teenager
in its north window

                    Your feelings
were barely decent enough to cover
your skin   They were the texture
of dirty gardenias   They smelled like
frogs on a humid summer night
when the air is locked into
a bedroom

                    Your feelings
lacked Rudolph Valentino   They were
too dogeared to suffer all those
pedestrian crosswalks, always got hit
by kids on tricycles   The price
for your feelings was a paper airplane
which won't fly more than 10 feet
above smoke level

                    You don't regret
the sale   You are lying on a waterbed
in your bedroom, lofted in
reverie   The garage was sold too
You invent one feeling
then another and so on   Each one
is stored away in the holds of air
You lazily search the classifieds
for another garage

Rousseau's "The Dream"

That redbreasted, blackwinged bird
gazes serenely eastward at something
not shown. A naked woman
on a couch in the clotted forest
of blue, pink and yellow flowers,
and green leaves of assorted shapes,
gazes in the same direction as the bird.
One lion with menacing eyes
peers out from lush vegetation
at the spectator of the painting.
The other lion, also with fiery eyes,
stares at the woman's upraised haunch.
A moon-colored sun, or the moon itself,
is clearly visible, though hemmed in
between two clusters of dark green foliage.
The spectator's eye wanders from here to there,
uncertain. Where is the action?
Of course, there is none. What moves
in the painting is the outer eye,
the one that is not inside the dream.
This eye, off to the east, looks into itself,
its own delirious bursts of color,
which the redbreasted, blackwinged bird,
during all this time, has been coolly observing:
this other dream struggling out of its night.

White Panther

I camped last night in the ravine
northeast of Taos where the white panther
was rumored several times in recent months.
During the night I was counseled twice,
once by footfalls outside the tent
and later by an Indian, tall and hatchet-nosed,
eyes brown and calm as a bear's.
He said, "Get up and look outside."

I opened the flap and there was the moon,
stony cold, slanting through my dream.
The spruce and pine were still.
The fire I'd built to cook my late meal
was a grey cloud of ashes.
I remembered the footfalls and thought,
"Of course, it was the white panther!
God has consented to believe in me."

When I awoke in the morning
a crow had gotten wedged into my chest.
His wings smashed about furiously
and his "caw-caw" was the voice
of the Indian laughing at me.
Despite his counsel I had slept through
my welcome. There is no white panther
northeast of Taos, not any more.

Soulfeathers for Albert Camus

In Albuquerque "the relentless
bad taste
        reaches a point of baroque extravagance
where all can be forgiven"
                The miles
of neon lights along Central Avenue
attract me as no other lights anywhere
I'm a tourist
        nothing more
of this nightly bawdy passage
through the New Mexico plains

Albuquerque is a desert
             During the day
I can be alone with it   I can make love
to it   How can it resist me
helpless as it is   a city of little character
and no repute?   All it asks of me
is that I bring back flowery stories
from Santa Fe
        60 miles away
Santa Fe is a bitch   We would quarrel incessantly
There would be questions of fidelity

Relationships

When you say the clouds
are your special friends it is not
to disown the desert sun
this most luminous enchanter
for whom you bear your life
in a suitcase
          The clouds are
a respite and a seclusion
You converse with them alone
at a table in the dingy smokehole
of a bar   The clouds inhabit
a can of Coors as easily as
any other space
          When you
lug yourself along under the sun,
that crisp sun so high a swinger
in New Mexico, there is always something
you leave behind   a forgotten
story   a wise caution
You neglect yourself   as if you were
a strip of celluloid
            When the clouds
come around you can tell them this
they know what you mean

"Goodbye, Loves"

for David & Mona Johnson

SAN FRANCISCO (UPI)—A 20-year-old hippie, high on drugs, shouted "Goodbye, Loves" and jumped the 275 feet from the Golden Gate Bridge into San Francisco Bay with his sandals in his hand Tuesday. He came up singing from a plunge that has taken 364 lives.

1 Truchas

These clouds do not conclude

They are indigo, gray, in portions unwashed
white   yellowish substrata appear
as windows of dried sweat in the sky over
Truchas   It is a late-afternoon hour of
mourning   for what, none of us
can say   Perhaps it is we ourselves
who mourn for those irresolute agencies
moving slowly through our eyes
disguised as clouds

               As we entered
the town we met a torn building
black from burning   small windows /
skull's eyes   A one-lane main street
thinly layered in asphalt
                   Fernandez
the garage-man told us where
White's gallery was "go down there about 7 blocks
               the Presbyterian Church
               a picket fence
               20 feet high   only one in town"

      WHITE'S GALLERY
         VISITORS
        WELCOME
      —————>

This town was Toledo   horizontal and
brown adobe   It was
Spain
        brown vision of Spain
the penitent eyes   under the marshals
of heaven, hoary, holding splintered batons
"electrified" (as today's tongue
consumes the spiritual field off
in the distance
                    O specters
children smiling
                    your teeth small white clocks
that themselves don't know
what time it is)

2 Lama

They welcomed us to Lama with
communal smiles   (This place a domestic
physical moon   men bearded   women
in long skirts)
                    and offered us
home-baked bread spread with goat's cheese
alfalfa sprouts
                    An ex-Marine corporal
Eric
        filing a curved chunk of branch
gripped in a vise explained
the 5:30 a.m. bell for voluntary meditation
the bell at 6:30 for imperative planning
breakfast and to work at 8
                            building
the women cooking 3 meals a day for 30
in evening dancing and chanting
                                the ashram
not yet structured the dues not yet

regulated hours of labor to equal 7
which could equal 6 or 5 as to
one's ability   not to be codified

Paraphrase:
          "Physical dominant over spiritual now
              as to our nascent need"
The brochure:
              "It should be understood that
              Lama Foundation provides only
              the rudiments—tools and working area
              What the individual makes of them
              will depend on
                          the sort of energy
              he is willing to commit
              to this effort   We emphasize
              the extraordinary difficulties
              involved on all levels
                          of this work

Eric
        blond muscular   eyes voyaging
toward the earthly moon   shaping a twisted
bit of branch into something   whatever
humanly necessary   The black girl said
"He's beautiful used to be
                    in the Marines has
the discipline"
              Part of a play written /
the labor in his hands, gloved
smoothing down the wood

              "We realize that for something new
                to be born
                          something old
                must die"

Those who would live on this
moon above Taos
                         should speak to themselves
honestly

3 Truchas

Sunlight at 9000 feet unimpeded strikes through
to the vein streams down the mountains
of the brain across the brow
into prophetic sight   white shadow
is monolithically black no light refracted
intense opposition to prisms
which comprise the heart   in one day
we met Manicheus face to ass

The Trouts is airless Lama perhaps
all air
              White's gallery was an open
crypt the body punished to salvage it
for Jesus' mercy   self-taught paintings
had learned the ropes and whips, the chains
that thrash and lead a man to his personal
Calvary   union in pain with One
Who spared Himself none
                                    White himself
no angel in the Body of Christ but an Anglo
detached enough to bear a lantern
into the coffin where the town's Penitentes
prayed as he listened to the Spanish cantor
chant the *albados* in praise
of the Holy Sacraments   singing in his gut
the same stanzas White long white hair
near his heart the six-shooter   silver bullets
scattered throughout his head

St. John of the Cross:

> I live without inhabiting
> Myself—in such wise that I
> Am dying that I do not die

The *morada* "is easy to identify because
it is usually long and low close to
the earth   Its length usually several times
its width shaped not unlike a coffin
Its massive walls are of hand-textured adobe
giving the structure a unique organic
sculptured quality   It is the essence
of simplicity in design"

Truchas confined to an old fever dozes
through its days
                     (these clouds
do not conclude)
                      at night in heat
squirms and turns on its cliffside
torturing itself to
   in one violent motion
                            in one last straining
ecstasy
           drop from the Sangre de Cristos
to the dead far down

"Their dead march with them
in the Paschal season   They require no Easter
The Resurrection is present in their tapers
their flutes clackers maracas and
occasionally a drum"

4 Lama

Whom to believe?
                The head lightens
and is held in a leaf   Earth swells
in its pod
          10 lbs of peas
at this height
            Lama
onions alfalfa lima beans   water trickling
into the gully steadily
                  and the head
enters a green album   arranged
pictures of love torn from the wilderness
and we look
              into the eyes of a goat

Out of sullen streets of individual
existence rises the dome of assertion
To the solar eminence these people address
their letters and craft   They ask of You
warmth Your flowering radiance
aware that You are purely there insentient
a keg of fire   bodiless unagonized
We pour Your golden blood into our spirits
get drunk on sheer light
                And Christ
is a dead man whose presence here
consumes the pagan passion   rites
of soil tribal paternity worship of
the clouds
            that do not conclude

Those who depart, to California or
India will return
            Who are the dead

but ourselves?
                    Observe a radish
dip a finger into mud
sit on a log   You have achieved
life and henceforth walk among
the godstruck   Hard on this hillside
they hollow wholeness out of absence
Calm is king in the hushed claims
of holiness
                    Rapture is death
Those who drink goat's milk
are bones in the meadow of Krishna

If they hold to their course
there is an Orpheus for everyone

5 Truchas

Finally to arrange these distortions
if they are   Your years of crime
pour through your bandages   There are pools
of lilac and oregano behind your grimy
lids changing form as the blood charges
through its circuits as the nerves
close in upon the horses prancing in the lamplit
streets   It is night in the tabernacle
where the years' catch of wounded lie
Poor fish they are! fetid and rotten
Who could eat them
                              or lick
such wounds
                    Arthritis has whipped
Mr. White into a hump a hunch
Art has fattened him (his primitive guess
at the poison in his bones buried in the mounds
under the prison of his
brain) And he said:

They bury their dead in the ground
of their church   and when the dead
grow too numerous they stuff the bones
into the adobe walls   After many rains
when the walls have been washed thin
a thigh or arm reaches through
projects into air   (again the air)
groping for air   So many bones stick out
so many pegs a man could climb them
all the way up to the cross

White says he has died already
he has nothing to fear
                              not even
the Postmaster of Truchas
                              his town's
chief political figure and foe

"I know who stole my files"
"I'm going to paint flowers on my kitchen window"
"Monday I'll go to his house
with my gun"   "The kids raise hell at night"
"It's so peaceful here"   "The smart ones
move away"   "They drive at 90 down the narrow
street drunk bang bang bang"   "I love it
in Truchas"   "If he doesn't return my files
I'll start banging too"   "They burned down
the hardware store in the April uprising"
"Emanuel is too nice"   "The Postmaster controls
the Welfare"   "You have to be ready
to shoot"   "It's a restful town the dead
are beautiful"

Aromas of earth   calm of the
nightworld insects in molecular whirl
ants and roaches at their duty
on pavement and dirt   Stare at them

long enough and you too crawl swiftly
among them one with such lucid striving
while higher the lamps swarm harshly
into dark air   They do not help you
to see / the eyes are trained to motions
beyond light the heart waits in shadows
it waits for a garden to bloom
out of song as the song enters the Savior's
pierced flesh and the Mother of Sorrows
embraces Him ah! their gloomy love
You stand holding your breath in
your fingertips the rain runs down
your cheeks all you remember
is the island where you were young
the fruit on the trees the sap glued
to the bark   You begin to walk
and walk until the dog announces himself
turn back drenched by the years
bitten by teeth that surprise you
from a distance   Do you Believe?
In nothing but sun and moon
in what they have accomplished by their incessant
turning as you have stood
alone in the night
accepting your own presence fully at last
a youth again   The lady with golden hair
who emerges from the doorway
is surely a goddess

6 Lama

Tammuz and *Ishtar*   the Cult of Life
returns from Christ's agony
formed as a child who eats
the goatcheese
                    of the new moon

"Where the grass was not, the grass is eaten,
　　Where water was not, water is drunk,
　　Where the cattle sheds were not, cattle sheds are built"

The clouds do not conclude
but open heaven again for the pagan
goddess the youth's mother his sister
his lover

　　　　　Christ the fallen King
dies forever the church is fallow
His embassy closed   We cannot relive Him
with our suffering   He will refuse to sip our blood
at our last supper preferring as always
a fried catfish
　　　　　　　The dead merely stretch their arms
outward from the earth's moon and grasp
the rains of spring to serve our eyes
that survey so curiously the surface of things
The dead have been here before
and lead us into that memory through which
we must newly pass
　　　　　　　Deliver us
Adonis from the darkness of Hades
Gentle youth   long brown hair brown eyes
beloved of Aphrodite   wounded early
dead too soon   O Lazarus in maroon doublet
and cardinal leotards healed
it must abstractly be said
　　　　　　　　by beauty
that whispering song of our skin
How lovingly we fuck with nature
when Adonis ploughs the seed of our phallus
and Aphrodite harvests the swollen grain

I structure our most ancient epic into
personal terms

                    Handsome and profound source
first prince of my annals:
my own son almost 7 My daughter
somewhat older and cooler
                              oracle
of my only temple
                    There is a man
there is a woman
                    a child is born
No faith outlives the order
of this procedure
                    Then quickly
while the wind holds me in the cup
of my singing fall   as I pretend to be
Icarus tripping headlong toward the wise

embrace of the sea I flap my sandals
flap flap
              in air
                        my long hair
pulls me back skyward I'm in the middle
of a marriage I'm the center
of incomparable solace I originate
and I conclude
                    I ee why ee   eye am
swimming among fishes ready
to rise again to the surface
                              to humor every crisis

That is the lyric that issues me
firefly wings the shiny
beetle coat "America the Beautiful" the flying
hippie sang, after death Of course of course
another strophe another stroke

The Intellectuals at Okie's Bar

for Gus Blaisdell

They are lovers of their own distortions
who sit in such darkness   music
steaming about them
                        beer swelling
their muscles / sense and temperance
tortured into hours of speech
to dowse their minds' reflection
                            Ocean at night
leaps up in tongues of green illuminated
spume   and dies on sand
A residual humor flaps its wings
evacuates into air
                    The bar is
headquarters for difficult gymnastics

There is nothing outside but stars
and a sliced moon   cold now in November that
arrogant Heaven peopled by the dead
Cars wearing holsters cruise
the boulevard
                    at one with those harmonious
seasons and cycles to which
the balls of drunks aspire:
                            to be contained
in Purpose   molten fluid pouring
through strict cylinders
                        to arrive at
the laurel bush at last   completely relieved
done with hessian duty   into the arms
of a goddess more woman than ghost

We are not the mob that coils
around Fortune's rim   Snake eyes
inhabit our bones
                        seeing fumes
canopy all happy processions (prophesy also
the pit where brains are buried)
                                        so we refuse
to march
              hippity-hop through Hell instead
our toes quick
              as red coals
spend our laughter in heads of foam
matching the need for bright occasions

Placitas Night

for Steve Katona and Neil Nelson

How   as you walk from
                                this moon
that casts a shadowy oval
    on the cloudlit sky
leaving the car stuck in earth
                as you cower
                        under the moon
you are one candle
among stones
    a sputtering on two feet

There is no word

Behind / retreating from
        a silverless mine   home for
        snakes gophers moles of the ages

You are heading toward

The way you came down
has not held its ground   it has
not waited
                The moon
holds you to its chart
    Holds
            you run
                        Soon

It comes   in this lost plot
a nowhere
                the gathering up of all
comings & goings
You are together at last
with yourself   The wings in your gut
strain at the walls   they can't get out
they'll never
                Slow   slowly
you know
                that the moon
has entered your life   You go on

Stanford Street Poem

When living
            even with people you love
boils you dry each day
                        what music shall
calm you   Can the sky open *that* wide
to receive your cry

                    The gag of love
steals your tongue   what you know
of soil and sea   flowering and fall

As other bodies call to you
a woman's teeth a man's beard
you approach them   cold leaves in your legs
leaning on an old moonbeam
                            the song:
a single crow on the naked bough

            snow on the Sandias now
            creamy fields below Taos

            water in hose will freeze

            nothing   to reach for

you must
            dance
                    with the trees

After Reading Some Poems
by William Bronk

One languishes inside the local custom
of a world. As if tomorrow will come
without clothes, tailor's dummy stuck with pins;
in a corner of the formless, some bolts of cloth.
Not that we lack source or spirit—
what we have is too much world.

One cuts into blue and snips out
the figure of a memory, a sky
on such-&-such a nameless day. We sew on
yellow eyes, a nose, a mouth, and so it's done,
the doll of sky. This is the real world,
the one that is in doubt. One gives it

a name, out of indifference or ennui,
or perhaps because identity is nothing more
than remembrance, a time buried in the tongue.
How to crush this habit! One travels elsewhere,
builds board by board a tiny house
under different stars, slips into fresh

habiliments, starts drinking papaya juice every night
before sleep. Dreams march through
at a brisker cadence, friendships grow like beets.
What was thought to be loneliness
now is seen as prolific solitude
dubbed with voices, with desired faces.

One listens and hears, finally, in the next room
loud shouting about some abstruse thread
that draws us together—fear, love, the minotaur.
Apprehending ourselves in the world is a world,
for the time, being. Whatever we say is required,
could not be other, not for the world.

Correlating A Woman

for Halvard Johnson

1. I perceived myself falling in love
   in bits and pieces, in black and white.
   On page 20 she wore a floral robe
   loosely closed, her right arm extended over
   her abdomen, her hand veined, stark,
   in light shadow, a downward arc.

2. On page 21 this robe was slightly parted
   to show the arcs of her breasts,
   the space between them. A ridge of shade
   covered the right arc, perhaps fostering
   an illusion: that it was higher than the left.
   The right hand was perpendicular
   to the torso and held the left,
   fingers loosely intertwined. The fourth finger
   of the right hand wore a dark-stoned
   oval ring. A segment of ring could also
   be glimpsed on the other fourth finger.
   Below the hands, which concealed the navel,
   the woman's belly was bare
   but a white edge cut off her body there.

3. Page 49, a woman's back, naked,
   high arc of left hip, the right curved
   in shadow. Her arms ended at the elbows.
   A breast, or perhaps its shadow,
   protruded to the left between elbow and torso.
   Her buttocks ended at the beginning
   of their cleft, shaded to the left.

4. Page 64 provided the most extensive section,
   from bosom to knees, naked. The right breast,
   because of the angle, appeared to arch
   lower than the left, right nipple extended,
   left not visible. The navel much nearer

the bust than the pubis, possibly indicating
large, full breasts, sloping low. Certainly
a long expanse of belly, slight
in its mound. The pubic hair was dark
and dense, ending at the top in a straight edge,
probably shaved thus. If so, I wondered how tall
this hair might grow. The left thigh,
full and heavily shadowed, was forward,
preventing a view of the complete pubic arc.
Her left hand was braced lightly on the hip.
Yes, a ring on the fourth finger,
this one also an oval shape.

5. On page 87 was half the woman's face
or, at least, I assume this was
the same woman, since both hands, fisted,
thumbs extended, covered the mouth
and on each hand was an oval ring.
Eyes large, dark arcs. Anguished expression.
She wore a black top. High forehead,
hair long down each side. She was
clearly modeled for her sensuous fashion.

6. Page 97 was the last meeting. Again
a facial view, hair wrapped in a towel.
Eyesockets wide, almost hidden in shadow.
Nose long and full, lips heavy. Her fingers
branched widely across each side
of her face, a stylized Hindu goddess.
Her sexual arc remained, as before, hidden by design,
once more the oval rings quite plain.

The Moon at Canyon de Chelly

Tonight the moon is limned on a slanting wall
of the White House ruin in Canyon de Chelly.
Centuries ago a different moon
bleached this same wall, perceived by the *Diné*
as a story to be told at dawn.

Tonight this moon is not a story.
It is a law. Still, its composition on the wall
at Canyon de Chelly recalls that private moon,
the first each of us ever saw. Though the pueblo
is dead we hear the story its people told.

This moon drains the brown and gray,
the ocher and pink from the earth. It whitewashes
everything. That is what it does.
Now as the sun returns to us at dawn,
we see the moon was only pretending.

They did not say it so. It is someone among us
who, recalling some private moon, having forgotten
its names, pretends to hear its echo here.
And we all do that, call out in our own voice
to our oldest moon, this one on the cliffside wall.

Stages in Assembling a Mirror

*The Renaissance explores the universe;
the baroque explores libraries.*

WALTER BENJAMIN

*A[love]relationship is as "real" as one's
willing to fictionalize it.*

CARL THAYLER

I. The Opening Shot Kills a Dead Bird

Triangulated, the crosshaired eye
pleads for smooth air, assent of sun
and the victim. The eye sees two nuthatches swoop
into a sycamore stand and creep along the limbs
hunting small crawlers.
                            What can be seen
is positioned, the sudden surge of a warbler
wedged into an angle of the air.
The eye, crosshaired, fires in fourfold vision
focused on a mote, a note
wobbling on wounded stilts.
                            Hidden eye
perched behind a cloverleaf
watches the fall of its prey; blood spots dot
the air going down, and mizzles of smoke
blow across memoirs of this dawn's
tableaux.
            Hardly a shadow
cast yet by sunlight. Scratchings of a song
impinge on the eye's pulsing wax,
nothing more than a squawk in the air
refusing to die away. A vacancy seen
where the nightingale fled its glory,
for decades embalmed in gold, in golden duende.
The eye, triangulating, forced a new sound
into the trees.

Dreamed in four sequences,
this conjunction of flight and fall
is unlike any heretofore surfaced
in the cross of matches, as if the eye beheld
its sight gone out in striking Christ's body
too many times head-on. That churchly soul
blackened after too many flares of sun.

II. How His Fingers Begin with Scarcity

A fat child. Who would look at him
except to shine a funhouse mirror in his eyes
to laugh at his shape in the glass
as it gathered to itself, one eye of the sun,
beaming out? One begins with a misshapen image
between skin and air.

The fat child conceals his fatness
by wearing extra clothes, by always walking far from
his shadow, by stabbing pain with his nails,
by shutting eyes, pulling down window shades.
So this child walks the irregular path
around Bluewater Lake, perceiving it as a perfect circle,
and all water as glass, an eye which does not see
but reflects thinly, lovably. Birds are friends
because they fly from the hand. Dogs are enemies,
their fur too often crowds the human skin
with impatience, determined to breach the pores.

As in the comic strips, the child puts X's
where his eyes would be, indicating sleep
or loss of will—crossing out the air
that smells of lecherous fish, of saltpeter
and honeysuckle, of the perfumes
in which bodies bathe their discontents.
The child does not sweat, he dries year by year
into a witness for scarcity.

In adulthood, perhaps no longer fat,
he goes to an optometrist once a week for many years,
changing glasses as he goes, changing without regard,
needing only the magnification of his disease,
his sparrowy lust.

III. He Is Given a Role with a Heavy Eye

He orders the pages of his heart—
and another's, many others',
all bound perfectly together, stitched and glued;
these attachments, the seasons growing into one another
never to be separated, though each had
its pervasiveness in the sequence.

What does he know reading so much,
staring into the blaze where fictions
prolonged his interest in possible combinations?
The heart a figment of the real?
These pages speak love but they hate
or plagiarize hate, yet he cannot sever them from his eye
except by razor blade, scissors or the knife.

On the knoll above the lake
he sits watching children sail their boats.
How the children frown for the safety
of their craft. He saw one
reef on a mudpatch in the middle
of the water, out of poling range, and the child
wept, wept so loudly as if all his power
were lost aboard the beached vessel.
So real, the man himself studied to weep.

But somewhere it stopped, this restless
merging of eyes with objects,
including written forms of objects
which deserved attention only because

they spared the heart so seriously.
One loved the image
of one's desire—or the desire itself—
instead of its odor. He grew sick.
his eye a stone in the mind;
he spoke only with birds and the dead.

So he continued, a midnight scholar
and scholar of midnight, surviving as a supernumerary
in love's fiction. He remembers
useless tears unshed, saves them like coins in the bank.
He is too alone to matter, too much a child
waiting in one of the four dim corners,
waiting to be called into the light.
His eye weighs him down. The pages
stick together and his fingers grow numb
in their labor of squeezing pulse after pulse.

IV. A Compassionate Movie Starring
the Seeing of Blindness

He sees the paling lip of her beauty,
her eye waning in its white sauce, the egg
drowning in its water. His view is at a tender angle,
a slit in the whole moratorium
of her love for him. He is elsewhere,
riding his horse in a circle when she looks
through the spring in her eye.
He is cantering across the desert when she calls
for his witness to her crossing of sticks,
and he does not hear the rub of her cry across the sands.

They meet again of course. He is a reductionist
who subsists on the meat of a single inducement,
the tempting morsel, primal with scent and echo
of childhood's "because." Why because?
Because why. Cuz cuz cuz. For her, too,

the air tingling with romantic magnolia
is too beguiling to forget, so she breathes him in,
his eye-misting pollen, the hair of his horse's flanks.
Her mind is nailed to her body.

She takes a job in the chorus line
of *All That Jazz*, lucky to get it amidst
all that winsome competition. Is seen by millions
as a blonde young lady who takes off all her clothes
while the cameras watch, and he too. Watches.
She is strange to him. Something he remembers,
the blue scrap of her underpants, her eyes
and the innocent heavens. But that one died,
perhaps in some cage for the criminally lovely,
the loving ones.
                    What remorse, then, is the use
and how to believe there once had been
an interplay? He leaves the theater
only to realize that she remains
inside.
            From where she has also
recognized him, as a stranger, one face
diminished by time, disordered in the throes
of too much sex, or too little. As she strips
before him in the movie house, reducing herself blind
to a few squares of film for his memory to recover,
she grows ill, vomits up heart and lungs,
even her genitals, until she is a framed vision,
no more than what he saw, what dwells through him
like a dream or virtue. To be so blindly reduced!

V. He Listens for the Double Song

When she sang her voice rose
higher than the tallest hedges, it overcame
such resistance as the air could muster
as its most austere point of defense.

Her singing not only accompanied the landscape,
it inhered in snails, pebbles, crabgrass,
the bark of trees; it forced upon the neighborhood
a continuous, disturbing sound
before her voice was assimilated,
like resin, into the pores of heavy, almost human, air.

She rivaled the crickets,
the continuity of her voice humming
over hedges, ascending above rooftops
filtering into the Byzantine leaves and glosscoated boughs
of the barest months. What matter that her songs
migrated from Appalachia or fled
from the false time of Tin Pan Alley?
If she had a name, no one knew it
or even where precisely she lived,
which apartment, what church she attended.

Some residents complain within a three-mile radius.
The police are called. They fire shots
into the air but only a few feathers
float to earth, bloody gold, white, blue,
bloody green and black. Her voice grows deeper,
it grows in shadows, more wisely,
at moments frenzied. Then, if one listens fully,
another voice in high register
reprises on "Jesu, Joy of Man's Desiring,"
the same voice returning to its source in rain
or wind, in golden apples or a butchered pig.

VI. He Imagines Another Life, De-Familiarized

It's not the woman problem alone. A man
is his own minotaur, he threads an opening bewitched
by the furious antecedents of dreams, his own
and those of his makers, the mothers and fathers

who marked their graves with their hieroglyphs.
That man who opens his arms to phantoms
is the apostle of his undoing.
Not woman but warfare's milky thread
leads him through cycles of dismembering stars
toward mercy in fragments
and the keen blades of appetite.
                              He arrives
at her house always a little late, always
a guest expected but slightly forgotten.
She is kind and allows him to enter. Do come in.
Yes, do. The lights are dowsed in preparation for sleep
and he can see that she is drowsy. So late has he come,
after midnight.
                    But my dear, can't we pretend?
And yes, they sit side by side for hours
on the sofa, holding hands, saying hardly anything.
The lights by now are barely visible,
darkness flavors the house
like elderly spinsters taking tea. He cannot leave.
Too many clouds roll in gray masses into his eyes,
thunder descends into his veins and arteries
and he shudders, the low, rumbling storm
sprouting its horrifying petals in his lungs.
It must be that he is in the wrong room,
else why is he suddenly alone? Why do the moments
sleep in his arms with such formidable death?

He manacles himself to the streets,
lurching toward home under a stale moon,
half-devoured. If he could still love her—
as if he ever did. Leonine sun. Bull of the moon.
The door he kicks ajar, the bed he brutally falls upon
no longer familiar. Some beast snorts outside in the hallway.
He must dream the morning once more into emerald being,
she beside him unclothed, burgeoning.

VII. The Twilight Is His Lover

Yet he does not dare adopt her point of view,
or try to. As de Beauvoir said,
she is the Other, ironically—woman, not hehimselfness.
For whom he plays on the lyre, chords,
strungout guts vibrating more swiftly
than their mechanics should allow, chords
he wrongs by playing at his own standstill pace,
his fingers left vibrating the air.
                                        Better than
the gun. His affliction, to be lifebound
with those drools and whimperings one remembers
from observing twilights in Hades.
Last night he drove to a party in the North Valley,
alongside him the depleted sun continued
to follow baroquely:
first, the ghostliness of gold absorbed by a citron fringe
shading into a pale rouge; second, the philosophical gaze
between blood and poets' corrupted azure, alchemized
into a radiant bruise, muscadine so pure
it cannot grow anywhere in earth.
Finally, the dispersement into conventional
purple and indigo.
                            Or it might have been
another night, the woman's night, which calmed
his yearning for the possible. He would not belie
this portion of his nature, the lyre upon which
his untempered fingertips stirred melody
without hearing the friction of this process.
If even for a moment he might be Orpheus,
then he might also be Psyche's Lover:
soul and mind entwined like a moebius vine
in some god's riddle.
                            Enchantment, fury. Twinned
to ray out in manifold disguise, does he believe so much
truth? Better than the gun, with which he began
his accountancy in eyeball country, finger

latching to the trigger in this harmonious land
of pampering hands and danger. He will not
count his unclocked selves, he will rest
in reverie before and after each demand of power.
If he is not yet reconciled, the speech
of many voices at the party, for which
he prepares to leave his house, will conflate
soul's prospects into one more instance
of what he calls his migratory eros.
How he, when he speaks to this Other, wings the universe!

VIII. Sex, as Imaginal Center,
Stirs Memories of Wartime Newsreels

Sweet basil and dark moss.
His death already done, only the dying remains to do.
Crosshairs fuzz before his eye, four triangles
meet at one opening on a fleshy hillock,
one soaking mat of human hair. The shot
begun in youth still whistles in his ear,
reverberates in his bones, the first luring nightingale.
That shot flares again with unexpected lightning.
And her body, whatever its fresh form, shakes
as the clouds of his two skies collide,
shakes when he folds his reason into halves
and quarters from which the future extends
like a genealogical tree, each part consorting
with a root of his memory.
                              He calls a friend
to ask what to do in his dying. How lonely
to believe in time's radiant and deadly pollen,
perdurable flak blossoming in the heavens
where bombers hum once more in the Second Great War
and his violence misbegets a beauty
for whose image he murders truth.
Pathological, his friend says. A dream, he counters,
vaporous as a dream. Soul is just so frail,

wisps of smoke trailing the flights of eye,
so fiercely lodged in crystalline atmosphere afterwards
that their invisibility can never be erased
from his mind.
                        She knocks on his door every night.
You thought I was dead but I'm the ladybug
planted in your heart. The world can listen in, you know,
on how we live together. All that hiding,
the secrets and pretenses, and always the very heart
minutely documented. Asleep or awake, winds of desert or mountain,
great hurricanes sweep through mapped eye and ear,
leaving a landscape of obscene photographs.
And the morning blanks out all such traces,
clothes the eye in fashion
cut many decades before out of pure and primary colors.

IX. Finding a Body for Her Name

Bare breast lightly touches bare breast,
the woman's eyes closed or almost closed
as if both merely dream their desire. And he,
enchanted by the name "Nusch Eluard" (the white woman
in the photograph), cannot desist from inventing her
more than he does the actual figments of women.
Landscape and remembrance, a woman without boundaries
who existed for him in a pond of blue swans, in a sky
unfurrowed by wounds. Nusch (wife of the most delicate
Surrealist), a romance the fat knight (as he thought himself)
carried behind his visor for thirty years.
                             The shadow of a bird
flutters across his pillow. And she springs
into a life he did not imagine, a woman suddenly bodied,
double-sexed. In another picture she embraces
the shoulder of a Sapphic blonde woman, forehead touching
the other's cheek: in a moment they will kiss,
and he will turn the page to Nusch nude in shadow,
back and buttock curving in faint, graceful light,

anointing herself in the pose, the camera, 1935.
Her name beats with a rush of blood through his entire
chain of armor. Through a trick print of image
he overlays his body on hers, becomes her third,
black Ady, or Sonia or another already absorbed.
Then fourth, since he who loved her in fact (Eluard)
still superimposes his form from the shadows.

Transported by these pictures to Paris or Provence,
to medieval adultery, forensic under the lens' law,
he edits himself, brings along in his portmanteau
a heavy troubadour's assemblage in fever with our times:
the adored one stained by a carnival ink, phallus growing out
from a nipple, to be sucked off by practiced
and elegiac teeth. Pink rose afloat in waterhair.

A wind passes through his heart, he ascends
from the slaughterfield (all those dead tanks,
the rusted grass), he feels like a small planet
wavering in air, eyes whitening in space, the oven of space.
Remembrance and landscape. Even with his pain he loves
the blue ball of himself seen from a safe distance.

X. He Survives His Fate with Luck

Four, the male clover, reappears in his popular mind
as prefigurement of life surviving, doubling
its doubleness, then and now, now and then.
It is the diamond pitted in the heart, a hard
talisman that presses into the soft rind,
rounded to three, always the sacred receptacle,
trinity of birth, consummation and death.
The sum is seven, a meaningless number
stationed in the right place on the dice
and in the week of Logos' wonders.
                                    He is alone,
puzzled by zigzagging fish in water, birds

that float through the air with natural piety,
and a light infusing the restaurant's rose window
with such blonde intensity that he believes for a moment
in absence incarnate. And this belief,
though it disperses, glows afterwards in the goblet
from which he sips wine. The golden braid
of a fugue twists its two loving ghosts
around his thought and he wavers between
these hallowed figures, opposing but just.
Chance and Fate: man in woman, woman in man:
Eros calls to Psyche.
                         To the word, the genetic name—
so turns again to her, she who one day
entered his office, gave him her firm, sweating hand.
Spoke of poetry, its crystalline logic
that tightens memory around its wound, holds it
in the grip of gauze. How she could spell out, if she could,
a deliberate three-four music, coupled in climax,
or dolphin sequence of sonnets freely formed from scarlet rain
and white, sterilized sun.
                         Beside him now, nearly healed,
she orders squab baked in an orange sauce.
What shall he have? Roast duck in almonds
and French onion soup to begin them both.
They are in Toronto just off Bloor Street,
but why? Wouldn't she rather be back
in Maui? Her hair takes the room's honeyed light
without questions, the same shade
of a different substance, which his hand can reach for
or covet in mystery, can write into the world,
the one he had read, through the years, as an alphabet born,
torn from his own dyslexia.
                         Dining in this moderate place,
they swallow one fine truth after another, drink
the fact of home from vineyards far across the sea.
When their tongues kiss, they taste the visible
and, for once, are faithful to common sense.

XI. His Dream Awakes Dressed as a Woman

Regenerated, then, in Psyche—often spoken but not possessed
by anyone, open wound and wonder of Cupid's healing rod.
Psyche unstains the glass of one idea and one idol
and of the ghost that hides in ambush behind the altars.
Feminized by ancient usage, Psyche is the fourth eye:
which gazes through itself to endure the two visions
of Janus—god of beginnings whose door closes in time of terror
and opens in joy—and love not one embrace more than the other.

This is godly! he cries, the man whose breasts
decline man's customary armor
and who stands off the boulevard, blind to the passing legions.
This is godly! he cries, to the street's dogs and cats,
to Hades' immortal horses,
himself the meat of her labia, his snakebody
entering her mouth, which is also his own:
by choice, by happenstance, by the humor of nature
and matrix of mythic symbolmongering.
To be procreative god, and goddess of the word,
to be so blessed in plumb of deepest earth,
flaming chariots streaking across the past
through Christ's cloudy ashes risen like the always-recurring bird—
all generations posed in mirrors
in multiples of the ordinary man-woman.
His penis pours out milk.

As I have raged so long against rage let the winds
bear my lamentations to receptive loam, let them flower
as blooded iron spikes, let them grow thinner in rain and sun
until a child's fingers can strum their harvest.
My song is to age one leaf at a time and, in this exact and sure
completion of nakedness, ungild the nightingale.

The Armada

for Anna Moya

My friend, the tattooed woman,
waits behind a screen. Outside
an armada sails for the shore beyond mind,
toward source and proliferation. I remember
the poet saying, "Who believes in dreams
must ascend the rain."
                        The ships outside
move on to their destination,
modest galleons with flags patched together
from worn Renaissance costumes.
                               The rains continue
seeping into the poet's grave, if he is buried.
Longingly he told me once, "If only I could see
the first vision. All others would be the same."
But like all the dead he died blind.
                            The canvas screen
portrays the surrender of the Chinese Admiral Ting Ju-ch'ang
to the Japanese after the Battle of Wei-hai-wei.
One surrenders and thereafter waits. As the woman does,
for me or another, it doesn't seem to matter:
she dreams of eating apricots
directly from the branch.
                            Now suddenly the ships arrive
and pass from history through the paradise
of sultry lagoons, pass into a minor shape
barely accessible to our human instruments.
The poet said, "You are a fool to be standing there,
your shoes filling with water."
Before the armada there was hope.

I allegorize the woman, my friend,
her eyes glazed with happiness to know
that when she awakes her skin will be brighter still,
a regatta of flags, and she will repose
on water, sailing out in fluttering sunlight. Outside,
far from me, the nectar already glistens on her lips.

What Was Left Behind

She remains herself so painfully
that her windowglass splinters. Shivering,
she sees someone shining into her. Her cry mummified
in dankest air, she appears, a white thought. On the stairs
a rustle of cloth or a bird
scattering leaves.
                    Later, when the sun's hair
darkens and the light inside
falters, a candle gasping, she renounces
the other. As if someone knows her,
as if anyone betrays her. That's how beauty
reaches into her eyes, as memory only,
the grafting of another skin.
                    Normally
no one would care that the stains
her eyes leave on objects cannot be removed.
As if, though, this particular bloody sliver
hung from a light-chain could cut off a finger,
someone would not listen to her tell
to the last eyelash that fear of being found,
that moving about of a mangled thought:
someone she knew once, who forgot her.
                    Now climbing
the stairs up or down in nakedness,
the spite of dry lusts, she passes in review.
A finch lofts from her hand, a movement beyond growth.
She passes in spider weave through the lanterns
of someone's watch.
                    The harm she does
reaching for herself no one denies
nor the beauty of her solitary angle.
Even though, brazenly, she leaves her name
so far as the sensual icefields, someone cherishing
a sound she has left behind, her canary's
song, as if she knew one,
betrayed by memory only on the early track,
a glaring eye beaming into flesh, someone bringing her
one moon, the self of self, the stick's end.

Jackdaw

Wednesday, first day of the new year,
sun already warm, out of season,
in this high desert city as I awake
from aging sleep, up and about then,
scavenging in the usual ruins. I feel glossy today,
black and beaked, a finger among the many
reasons for declining to live
so obscurely, in bleak towers, still exiled
as Jew and poet, as one who cannot bend much
toward others.
                        On this first day,
aloft on one wing, then alighting, I root at the grave
of my Prague ancestor who failed his life.
Or it failed him. How to compromise
the difference? That's why I tug at myself,
peck away at those voices in the grass,
their luminous earth-hunger.
                                        Halley's Comet
visible to the Earth's unsheltered eye,
but not today. The nights don't excite me
as in my youth. Now it's sleep sharpens
my pen, the round, zigzagging meters
of sleep.
                In his grave, my father,
much younger than I forever, lies unburdened
except for the tombstone over his skull.
He wrote books and stories, parables,
thousands of letters. A man of great reason,
from which he suffered more than from
his bleeding lungs. O, the breath falters
however one tilts the head or dismembers
the pecking order.

Bird-man, I say to him,
at last you are a feather of metaphysics,
a sweetener of darkest space. Our atmosphere's
loud blue dust no longer compels your ear to close
like a shell or your eyes to water in laughter.
I envy you, father Franz, even as I fly
outside the old year, into conversations
with kind friends, people who love me
for my little blue light, the desperate calm
which they think is a mind scrupulous in matter.
Please, uncle Brod, save my manuscripts
and instead of keeping one memorial flame lit,
I promise to send the heavens up in smoke.

At Such Times

At such times it takes almost nothing—
a sound on the map, a short adieu moving down
along the balustrade, something less
than a slideframe of anything. Seen in sepia,
she reminded me of love. Like long ago.
Like someone who laughed and vanished
in lavender.
                    At such times art punishes,
the victrola plays leftover Schubert—but she wouldn't
say "love", would she? unless she meant it.
And why not believe in such good luck,
why not, at such times? Imagine it.

But she is too young, too blonde,
too obsessed. Wind torments the hyacinth
some lover placed honestly on her windowsill in Carolina,
where her mother sings German camp songs
and she herself goes mad every summer.

Because she is a history stamped on whitest mind,
I have entered the age of Lust-for-the-Princess
and eat with my fingers. I hack
at palm fronds with my machete
to mutilate all tropical manners.
                              At such times—
after she has smiled once more into the molding sun—
I weep with unspecified pain.

George Ruth's Middle Name

for Jean Burden

In the dream I forgot
that George Ruth's middle name
was Herman.
        What does this imply
about the unconscious? That at the least
it forgets middle names.
        Dreams are not
perfect. Memory dies even in our sleep.
Death is a dozing sentry.
        The Freudians
would ask why I repressed
George Ruth's middle name. There are no
Hermans in my life.
        But baseball
is a game and I am its witness.
Dead heroes do not live completely
in my dreams. Strength
and speed give way to lacunae
and lapidary wishes. Henry Moore
is the master of my ego.

I want to sleep again.

        But too late.
The name contains its absent orphan,
whom I see again only when daylight
slips through the gaps in my window drapes.

By late afternoon I wonder:
Who is George? Who is Ruth?

The Singer of Manoa Street

Reading Isaac Singer, I spring back
into my Jewish body. I take notes
on my left palm in a strange script,
although I recognize the word "onions"
and also "strategic demons." From somewhere
a gust of wind passes through me;
it smells like exalted soup. Shall I sew
a yellow Star of David onto each of my
aloha shirts?
                    Clearly, I must stop
reading Singer. One short work of his
seems enough to bring God's absence
into my room. Soon, while I am alone,
someone will look into my mirror who isn't me.
I remember my father, my mother,
my wife, all well-rested in the soil
of our American republic. These memories
are scarcely ideas.
                    It is too late
to put the book down. I'll go on
in my short pants, the nice fat boy still,
walking the streets of Honolulu,
observing how little remains
of my past. Each year there is less,
each year a fresh body of knowledge
moves through my blood and says,
"I'm home now. Just let me sleep."

Of course Singer is not to blame,
his job is telling stories. If I feel
more Jewish, it is personal, not too serious:
what I feel these days is like
last night's half moon. But I still won't sign
the Covenant, which chose me so eugenically—
"You're a Jew, kid. Don't chase after shiksas."
I'll think more about Jehovah, Who knows everything,
and also about how sly and careless nature is.

Young Woman, Much Older Man

She called him afterwards, when the winter
had already turned gray, when the stars bunched together
in small herds. Love was not a choice anyone could make.
It could not be collected like taxes. Beyond the fence,
which separated his house from the park, stood foreign houses,
arranged in an oval, each with its own manner of speech.
Let the two of them, she said, begin a fire,
let his piñon logs warm them both.

This was afterwards, two years while moon
followed sun, nothing between them
except a spacious quietude. In love, middle age is guilty
of improvidence until proved wanting. His beard
whitened, streaks of chalk on a once black slate.
He was a bulk. He sat heavily, minding his thoughts
as if they were someone else's children.

When the first crocus broke through into light
neither of them believed the earth knew much
about flowers. They talked by phone across great plains
of wheat and shattered cars. Everything the heart imagined
was true. Everything they had said to each other
or left behind the door, listening in, could not be disposed of
easily. A dangerous waste, this science of caring.

They met again. Their eyes stared into the heat
and their words grew crisp shadows that would not melt.
Nothing was between them. They stood naked
in their secrets. Clouds like vague boats
drifted across that land they shared so abruptly:
their knowledge that nowhere is, after all, a far place.
They loved then. They planted roots in the trembling air.

Saturn Is Mostly Weather

Lying with her, watching the rain
pass through sunlight, I think about
the miles of love that lie
before me, her eyes are closed
and she breathes in slow waves.
I can hear the rain washing off
the plumeria leaves, cleansing the tall
dirty palms.
        The distance ahead
must diminish, love by love,
and I delude myself in making a mask
of some god's face to see through.
We cannot share the mystery, she and I,
our dreams do not believe each other.

Her eyes circle around herself,
her sun, in the black starlit space
under her lids. Awake, I can't help
her going, I can only listen to wet wheels
passing over wet light outside the window.

She will say my name and again
it will be someone else's. All those loves,
little suburban planets apart and bound
to my death, orbiting far ahead
in some still undeveloped photographs.
Meanwhile, if I am not in bed
beside this woman, I must be elsewhere
not hearing the suddenly awakened silence,
which I realize is the rain's deliberate
cessation.

More harshly the sun
streaks across the opposite wall,
and the shadows are harsher. Morning is late,
I am older, I don't want to shave
or even wash my face in the glass.
I will send her away; she shows up
only as a shade in my eyes' dim
and mustardy gaze.
                    Then her mouth opens
just a whisper when her face
rolls slightly away from me, so I hear
our separation as the last evidence
of a moth's wavering into the dark.
The cycles continue, nothing ever ends
completely until the gutters themselves
crumble into fiery mutilated air.
Her fingers twitch on my thigh
as if they had come from another land.

Origins

for Tony Quagliano

They are my tenants, these immigrants
who live in the apartment of my mouth,
who raise their common geraniums
on windowsills or the porch perhaps,
wherever the mouth opens out
to a worldly view.
                                    They came from forest
and seashore, with cultivated passports
or over the toothy fence.
It took me years to grow familiar enough
to let them stay, let them be as they are:
poor albinos, cutthroats, career diplomats,
little caesars and big fools.
                                    They conceive
themselves with humility and much desire.
How they grow even after 50 years
in the same location. They go on
multiplying, miscegenating, crossing
the religious lines like fate itself.
And, dear lord of landlords, how they fight!
I have never gotten used to their bruises
and spurts of blood.
                                    Nor to
their bragging stinks, their pretensions
to pedigrees none of them has, nor to
the company they keep: librarians, sexnuts, romantics,
killers. All of them mixing together
in willy-nilly waylayings of my own good
mouth, which is American, with a job and BIC-pen complex
to prove it.
                                    They will never assimilate,
my tenants, those bastards. Let them be, I think,
let them do their worst. I don't even
talk their language any more.
I don't even collect the rent.

The Rain on Oahu

for Kaye Fredericks

Around 6 in the evening the first
drifts of rain land lightly on the rooftops,
the foliage and walkways of Manoa Valley.
Sunlight still shadows the eastern hills,
those green humpbacked fish that never swim
far from home. Sitting outside Coffee Manoa,
in the marketplace, I read about
Yamamoto, the "reluctant admiral",
who did a handstand once on a ship's balustrade
and later planned, despairingly,
the attack on Pearl Harbor. The coffee today,
a blend of Costa Rican and mocha beans,
tastes so friendly that I want to
shake its hand.

    Soon, back in my apartment,
I hear the rain drive into leaf
and rock. A waterfall, I think,
for the green fish to wade around in,
hidden under the surface of night.
I listen to Haydn, Mozart, Mahler
on FM—woodwinds, violins and rain.
Admiral, you were a warm-blooded man fallen among
sharks.

    Then, as every night, I hear
somewhere nearby an infant cry and cry in pain,
one cry linked to the next in a mortal chain.
These harsh blasts, like the heavily misted horn
of other days, weave a long alarm
over the rooftops. Then the dying out,
the quietness. Then again the bloodsoaked seeds
that infuse these mythlike islands
emerge under the ploughing skies,
wet green life sprung from deep holes.

In sleep I repeat the rain, the peat-peat of drops
on roof and leaf, the admiral's eyes flashing
on and off, still news in my watery film.

Weather and the Quiet Stars

After she painted the bathroom walls black,
she felt an easing in her hands, which often
flew about, fingers flapping, birds trapped
in a room. By their own foolishness,
trapped. She needed cleansing from the dirtiness
that lived a life of its own
between one breast and the other.
                                        Trade winds
sway the long-necked palms, a fishing boat
keels over near Molokai. All the news
gets soaked in the downpour. She listens
for the gecko's quick click on the white
bedroom wall. The entire house wants
to swim away from her.
                            Her hands hold on
to the lesson of poverty, the waiting on tables,
the wiping up after old folks in the restless
home. She thinks her heart inhabits
a greenhouse where all the degrees are warm
and steady. Her hands grow petals
that fall away at her look.
                            The lush islands,
more isolated than anywhere, do not
trust her. They watch, murmur in their old
volcanic tongue, conspire to wash her
into the sea. Outside, the now drizzling sunlight
swirls in the wind, almost snow, almost
another age. She thinks how time
is a waste, nothing she can fill in
with redheaded birds any more.
                            Weather
and the quiet stars tell her paradise
does not come cheap. She must contribute her life
to a more beautiful thought
than any she could think. Her wealth, her charm
lie in her chest, heavy, a dirtiness against
the overarching, all-gathering soul. Humming Walt Disney,
she painted on, painted her bathtub black.

Above Taos

Above Taos and north of Questa
the stream rounded slowly
through that year's October curve.
After our drive to the clearing
surrounded by oak and aspen, we spread
our old picnic blanket. I laid
some cans of Bud under the water
in that afternoon's gathering shades.

What I remember best is how the cold
cold beer shook my tongue awake.
Since then, during the years
when love was shriveling like words
soaked too long in air,
I have come to claim with greater
longing the still-bronze leaves
above Taos, the cool sunforce

spinning through tangled branches,
that stream's delicate wet brush
lapping at my ear. I have not
been back but think to find
that place again. If it too has not vanished
in time's erosion: the buried affection
and speechless leveling, the earth gone flat
with too much stale, neglected air.

Maps

That strength to be alone, she possesses it
like a tool. She invented a bronze moon
to hang over the city at night, to reflect not
the sun but its own immanence. I think to
judge her work seamlessly.

When the city retires
from gossip and swizzling, she imagines it
as the public place of her dream life. A trans-
positioning of limits. The city's maroon brick
buildings, still rich in old wealth, against
adobe.

She maps tirelessly an underground system
of intimacy: the Body Shop where the Moon
Goddess is reborn; no more Eve
in the Snakepit. Art, she says, is the sanest
illusion. Gazing into her moon, my eyes read
the shadows as pomegranate juice,

prescribed
for aborting unwanted little gods. That's my imagination
racing too far from her creation. Even as she
buzzes through the city on her motorcycle,
wearing a tux to Louie's Bar and nothing at all
to La Posada.

In her city, under the moon,
no opposition exists between naked and clothed.
No good is not evil. God has no name, neither is He
unknown: He is the Mother principle, haven
of all signs and significance, which we understand
via the diagram of our bones.

Our questions, she says,
are atoms in the rain. Our answers divide them.
She would have us live in a language
that contains itself like Ouroboros. To me
it's Elmer's glue, the white seasoning that shows
through the cracks in logic.

I use her shoulders

to stand upon, to see over simplicity the people's
representatives confronting each world as it happens,
their teeth clacking, dice on the table-top,
snake eyes and all the coziness of 7-11. Again,
I miss the joy in her evocation.
                              She's trying
to like herself better, to take the devil
in her lust. She builds the city with love
in mind, but it reflects her solitude, her need to be
secluded from others who thrust themselves into
all vacancies.
                    Her city walks its dogs
without a leash. Duchamp hides around the next
corner. She prefers mystery to a physical heaven.
Many bronze people inhabit her city, and many
of sapphire. She is the map of her motorcycle's
comings and goings.
                              She is the amazon who battles
the satraps of the Stock Exchange. I can't see her any more,
I can only hear her voice. It speaks and sings;
she is her own opera. She is an arrow always pointing
to the center: her own inwardness whose shadow casts her body
into transparency, through which her city comes clear.

The Metaphysics of Paper

Reading *The Confessions of St. Augustine*,
what impressed me most was the smell of humus.
Imbedded within the words, in each letter,
in each space between letters, was a wet sound,
not purely of water, wetness
that had impregnated woodpulp so the words
were heavy, rooted in some ancient tree
although the sound was aboveground. There was
in the saint's reflections a moist rigor.

As I listened, the words clung to air,
echoing the stolen pears from Tagaste
and a forest memory from Oregon.
So what I read on my lips was more
than the bishop wrote. The paper itself
revealed a long walk in a remote woods
where sunlight seeped through the higher foliage
only to be absorbed in layers by the soil.
How to describe God's truth by such

underfooting of His unimaginable substance?
Confessions are for bedtime after a spare supper.
The crickets rub lazily then race to catch up
with destiny, now as I run my hand
over the glazed legend on the book's cover.
Once more the clouds, green with earthworms,
wander through my eyes, I smell the caul in them
and believe no story except what grows
dankly clear, creaturely on my tongue.